WHEN I GROW UP I WILL BE A FUTURE LEADER!

The Storm Collection

Tempestt Lyles

Copyrights © 2025 Tempestt Lyles

All rights reserved. No part of this book may be reproduced, stored in a retrieval system, or transmitted in any form or by any means electronic, mechanical, photocopying, recording, or otherwise without prior written permission from the author, except for brief quotations in critical reviews or articles. The scanning, uploading, and distribution of this book via the internet or any other means without the permission of the author is illegal and punishable by law. Please purchase only authorized editions and support the author's work.

ISBN (Paperback): 978-1-963743-93-7

DEDICATION:

MOM
GRANDMA BETTY
GRANDMA MARY
PAIGE
MALACHI
LYRIC /
SUNDAE
CHLOE'
AMIR
IDRIS
MICAH
TRENT
ROSA
AMIR
BELLA BRYSON
ZACK
KAYDEN GIBSON
KHALANI MILEY
ZION
ISIAH
TYRELL HAGGINS JR.
SYDNEY
CODY
DJ
CHARLIE
RAYNA
CARSON
ZION
MADISON
LIL MAN QUE SOPHIE DUECE
MY UNBORN KIDS LIL BOBBI
UNCLE ANDRE AUNT MAE JAI' DAN
JAI' LIYAH ROGERS
NOVA
AUGUST FREEMAN
NYLAH JACKSON
GREY
NATALIA JACKSON
NATHANIEL JACKSON III
MY GODSON KAM
ERIN
MEL
MR. BOBBY (The best Teacher)
PANCAKE
NIKI GATLIN
MILAN
KEISHA
JAB JR.
ZION
AUNT SAN
KYLER
SEHVYN
ABBY

When I Grow Up I Will Be A Future Leader!

When I Grow Up I Will Be A Future Leader!

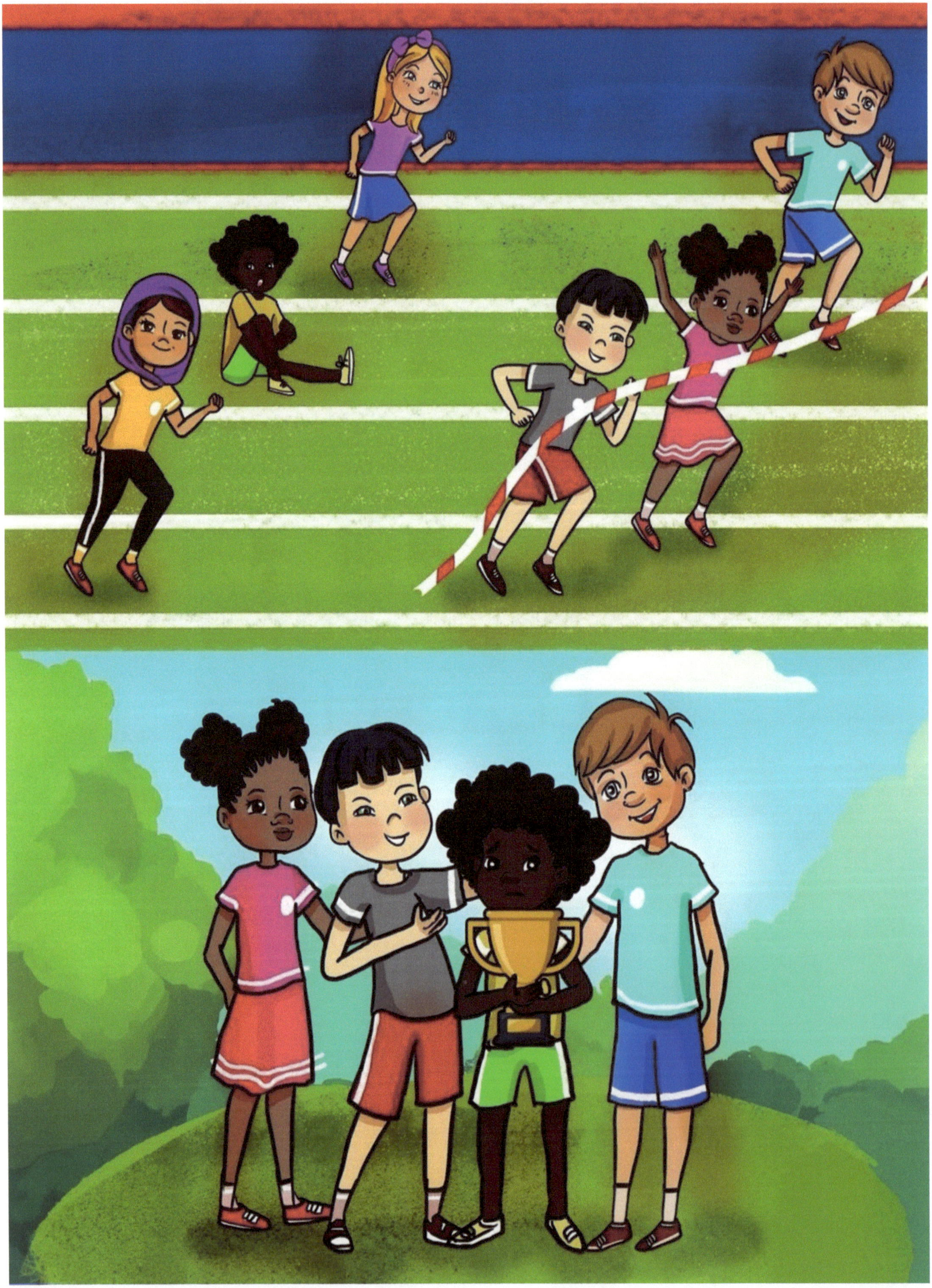

I WILL BE NICE TO EVERYONE, AND I WILL LEAD IN A WAY MY FRIENDS AND OTHERS WILL FOLLOW!

I WILL WALK WITH MY HEAD HELD HIGH. I WILL NOT GET DISCOURAGED WHEN THINGS DON'T WORK MY WAY!

I WILL NOT TEASE OTHERS, BECOME A BULLY, OR MAKE ANYONE FEEL I HAVE WRONGED THEM.

I WILL BE A BEACON OF JOY! LOVE WILL SURROUND ME. I WILL SEE NO ONE LESS THAN ME; EVERYONE WILL BE TREATED THE SAME.

I WILL MAKE A DIFFERENCE!

I WILL BE KIND!

I WILL THROW MY TRASH AWAY!

I WILL RECYCLE!

SMILE AND LIVE LIFE WITH A PURPOSE!

MAKE GREAT CHOICES AND TAKE THE RIGHT PATHS!

THE FUTURE LEADERS WILL MAKE OUR PARENT AND COUNTRY PROUD!

I WILL LEAD!

My name is Tempestt Lyles. I am 28 years old. I am from Thomasville, Georgia. I went to Busy Bear, Jerger Elementary, Scott Elementary, McIntyre Middle School, Thomasville Scholars Academy, Thomasville High School, and Thomas University. I love my city but I left to live in Orlando, Florida. Everything has been different and a challenge. I want to uplift everyone and make them happy. Love is real and starts as a child and grows into adulthood. I believe it takes a village to raise the children of today. We can all help our future leaders grow and develop. All children need love, and I love all kids. I dedicated my book to the children, and may my books go far! One change at a time. Growth is real, and it takes a lot, and children are watching us adults; we must give kids love and lead them right. They are our future leaders, and the training starts at home.

www.ingramcontent.com/pod-product-compliance
Lightning Source LLC
Chambersburg PA
CBHW042004150426
43194CB00002B/127